Birds of New Zealand

NGĀ MANU O AOTEAROA

collective nouns
ngā kupuingoa tōpū

Melissa Boardman

HarperCollins*Publishers*
Australia • Brazil • Canada • France • Germany • Holland • Hungary
India • Italy • Japan • Mexico • New Zealand • Poland • Spain • Sweden
Switzerland • United Kingdom • United States of America

First published in 2020

by HarperCollins*Publishers* (New Zealand) Limited
Unit D1, 63 Apollo Drive, Rosedale, Auckland 0632, New Zealand
harpercollins.co.nz

A catalogue record for this book is available from the National Library of New Zealand.

ISBN 978 1 7755 4165 3 (hdbk)
ISBN 978 1 7754 9196 5 (ebook)

Cover and internal illustrations by Melissa Boardman
Cover and internal design by Darren Holt, HarperCollins Design Studio
Colour reproduction by Graphic Print Group, South Australia

Printed and bound in China by RR Donnelley on 128gsm matt art

6 5 4 3 2 1   20 21 22 23

Introduction

As a youngster, I was always interested in animals and nature. My love for photography started early, too. I remember a book my grandparents gave me one Christmas called *Peter and His Camera*. Fascinated, I started taking a camera everywhere with me, documenting petting zoos, gardens and household pets. At university I studied design and photography, and found that during my degree I always steered my projects towards nature. I had a slow and heavy film camera back then, so taking photos of birds was all but impossible. It wasn't until I acquired a faster digital camera that I could begin to turn my focus to birds, and in particular native birds.

I really became enamoured with native birds on my first visit to Zealandia, a fenced, mainland ecosanctuary in Wellington. Walking into the valley was quite eye-opening: I saw birds I'd never seen before and some that I had no idea even existed. It's where I stumbled upon my very first toutouwai, the North Island robin. He was perched on top of a log and I was drawn to how undeniably cute he was and also how friendly he seemed to be. He didn't seem bothered by my presence and even hopped closer to me, which I wasn't expecting. When I got home that day I started to read about toutouwai. It wasn't until then that I realised how rare they are — they are defenceless against introduced predators and survive only in areas with intensive pest-control. These little birds, which seem so fearless and confident, simply don't stand a chance against the likes of stoats, rats, feral cats and possums.

I loved my visit to Zealandia so much that I started going more regularly, always with my camera in hand. Since the robins were friendly and easy to photograph I started to build up quite a collection of images. I began to create artwork based on them, originally with woodblock prints, then later with gouache illustration, which was my favourite medium.

I also incorporated other birds into my work, learning more about them along the way. The more I learned about how unique our native species are, the more I appreciated them and wanted to see them in the wild.

Today, many of our native birds are only found in specific locations and face a battle against a range of factors including habitat loss, introduced predators and human disturbance. Reading about the danger our native birds are in really made me realise what an amazing safe haven Zealandia is for our precious but highly vulnerable native wildlife.

As well as Zealandia, my home town of Wellington is also lucky to have Otari-Wilton's Bush, a stunning forest reserve which contains the nation's only botanical garden dedicated exclusively to native plants. I visit regularly and have learned a lot about native tree and plant species thanks to this wonderful place and its resources. The reserve is also home to a range of native birds, such as kererū (New Zealand pigeons), kākāriki (red-crowned parakeets), kārearea (New Zealand falcons), pīwakawaka (fantails) and more.

Thanks to both Otari-Wilton's Bush and Zealandia, Wellington has become alive with wildlife. Kākā can regularly be seen soaring through the skies and many gardens have much more birdlife than in decades past. Still, there are birds we'll never see without visiting a sanctuary like Zealandia, such as the 60 titipounamu (riflemen) translocated there in 2019. I began volunteering to help keep track of their distribution within the sanctuary, using my camera as a tool to try to identify individual birds and their behaviour. Volunteering has given my birdwatching trips much more meaning and purpose.

Since my first visits to reserves close to home, I have been fortunate to visit many other predator-free sanctuaries and offshore islands in New Zealand and experience nature as it should be. One of the most memorable experiences I had was in 2015, when I travelled to Stewart Island. I went on a kiwi-spotting night tour and spent two days on magical Ulva Island, where I encountered birds that I never thought I'd have the opportunity to see, such as mohua (yellowheads), pīpipi (brown creepers) and even a kiwi out foraging during the day (unlike other kiwi species, tokoeka, including the Stewart Island subspecies, are not strictly nocturnal). In the beautiful Marlborough Sounds I've visited the Blumine Island and Motuara sanctuaries, and have seen very rare kakī (black stilts) at the Ashley Estuary, just north of Christchurch.

In the North Island, I've been to Tiritiri Matangi Island several times, and seen kōkako up close, just a short boat ride from Auckland. I've been up close to kārearea (New Zealand falcon) at the Wingspan National Bird of Prey Centre in Rotorua, an organisation which does amazing work rehabilitating injured falcons and other birds such as the iconic ruru (morepork). I've also visited Sanctuary Mountain Maungatautari in the Waikato and Bushy Park Tarapuruhi, about 20 minutes north of Whanganui.

While I love getting amongst our native forests, I also love watching sea, shore and wading birds. I've been on a few seabird-watching trips and seen some amazing birds, from the majestic wandering albatross to tiny storm petrels that appear to walk on water. I love visiting estuaries and seeing dotterels, herons and terns. These types of birds can sometimes be overlooked as they're not as cute as some bird species, but they are just as important and worth celebrating.

While we treasure our birds, sadly many of them are now endangered. Introduced pests began to decimate birds in large numbers as soon as they arrived on our shores, and loss of habitat through land clearance meant many birds simply had nowhere to live. Many of our special native species are gone forever. Others have come dangerously close to extinction, surviving only through captive breeding programmes and innovative efforts by conservationists.

Although we can never recover our extinct species, there is plenty being done to protect the birds that we still have. Sanctuaries provide safe havens for our native wildlife, conservation efforts are protecting our most vulnerable birds and community trapping groups are helping to control pests in the suburbs.

I hope this book acts as a reminder to us all to help protect the habitats on which our native birds depend for survival. We have the power to save even the most threatened of birds on this list if we are mindful of where we tread, where we let our dogs and cats run free and how we can limit the damage of introduced predators such as possums, rats and stoats.

About the Collective Nouns

We are fortunate to have an incredibly diverse range of native birds in Aotearoa New Zealand. Over half of our native species are endemic — found nowhere else in the world. Their habitats range from dense forest to open pasture and everywhere in between. Some live mostly solitary lives, such as the albatross, which spends its life alone at sea, while some forest birds, such as silvereyes, live in social flocks year-round, travelling and foraging in groups.

This book features the collective nouns for many of our precious native bird species. A collective noun is a term used to represent a group of individuals as a whole, usually either people, animals or occasionally objects. Collective nouns first began to appear in the English language in the early fourteenth century, coined by hunters who wanted a fancy way to describe their booty. Since then, collective nouns have evolved and been absorbed into daily language. They are often humorous, such as 'an embarrassment of pandas' and 'a bloat of hippos'; dramatic, like 'a pride of lions'; or poetic, like 'a charm of finches'. Perhaps the most famous collective noun is 'a murder of crows', a term likely chosen because crows have historically been associated with death.

Many of New Zealand's native birds have been without their own unique collective nouns — until now. Our native birds are truly unique, so it makes sense that their collective nouns should be, too. It is much more descriptive to use a collective noun specific to a particular bird species rather than the usual 'flock' or 'group'.

The nouns used in this book reflect each bird's characteristics, whether it be their call, their colouring or their personality. Some have been adapted from terms used to describe groupings of overseas birds from the same scientific families as our native birds, while I have invented the following nouns specifically for this book.

'A cloud of whiteheads' refers not only to their white colouring, but also the way they forage high up in tree canopies, close to the clouds. They are often numerous and chatty, and in the nineteenth century forestry workers considered a noisy flock of whiteheads to be a sign that stormy weather was coming.

The whitehead's South Island relative, the yellowhead, behaves in much the same way, but it has striking yellow plumage. Their collective noun 'a bolt of yellowheads' refers to their bold yellow colouring.

Kākā are known for being cheeky and loud. As they soar above the treetops they can often be heard whistling and screeching, so 'a hoon of kākā' is a fitting collective noun.

The kea, the world's only alpine parrot, is a particularly cheeky relative of the kākā They are famous for destroying human property and getting themselves into trouble, so 'a circus of kea' seems appropriate!

A smaller parrot, the red-crowned parakeet, is known for its chatty contact calls that resemble laughter, hence the collective noun 'a cackling of red-crowned parakeets'. Similarly, the yellow-crowned parakeet are 'a gossiping of yellow-crowned parakeets', which reflects their call and also their secretive nature. They are often heard calling to each other, but are very well camouflaged in dense bush and can be hard to spot.

Another forest bird, the bellbird is one of our most talented songbirds, so its collective noun 'a ringing of bellbirds' reflects this. The bellbird's relative the tūī is also known for its song; they can often be seen singing to or at each other in close groups. A group of tūī is appropriately called 'an ecstasy'.

Saddlebacks have a different vocal range to tūī, and rather than singing melodic tunes they tend to chatter and chirp. Their name in te reo Māori, tīeke, is reflective of their sharp call, and therefore in a group they could be called 'a siren of saddlebacks'.

Stitchbirds are nectar-loving birds which require a rich diet that many sanctuaries in which they live can't provide entirely naturally. They often congregate around supplementary feeders, creating a busy atmosphere — so, 'a hive of stitchbirds' seems appropriate.

Fantails are named after their distinctive tails, used when hawking insects in flight. In the forest, they follow other birds around, taking advantage of the bugs they disturb. Because they can move and change direction rapidly their collective noun is 'a flutter of fantails'.

New Zealand's native robins are unusual birds in the sense that they seem friendly towards people. In the forest they will often follow walkers' footsteps, picking up any insects that are disturbed. In this book a group of North Island robins is called 'a rally', and a flock of South Island robins 'a company', both collective nouns reflecting their friendly nature and how they offer company to those walking in the forest. Chatham Islands' black robins are much more rare, but just as friendly. They have earned the collective noun 'a shadow', in reference to the way they follow people around and also their striking black plumage.

North Island kōkako have one of the most distinctive calls of any of our native birds. Their elaborate duets contain a variety of rich, organ-like notes, a call which is often described as eerie and haunting. Kōkako are also known as 'grey ghosts', which also contributed
to their collective noun, 'a haunting'.

Moreporks can often be heard calling at night. Their famous 'more-pork' call is most often a vocal duel between males, their calls back and forward earning them the collective noun 'an echo'.

Another famous nocturnal species group, the kiwi, spend their nights foraging on the forest floor for food. At different locations around New Zealand you may hear 'a rustling of rowi' or 'a rummaging of great spotted kiwi', or see 'a scurrying of little spotted kiwi', 'a burrowing of tokoeka' or 'a foraging of North Island brown kiwi'.

Weka are also flightless and look for food on the ground, but they do their foraging during the day. Around people they can get themselves into trouble by stealing food and belongings. 'A loot of weka' is very fitting for a group of these mischievous birds.

Rock wrens can fly, but they prefer to hop around on rocks, flicking their wings regularly. 'A flicker of rock wrens' is an appropriate collective noun.

Brown teals are a dabbling rather than a diving duck, and can be seen feeding on the water's surface. Therefore their collective noun is quite straight-forward: 'a dabbling of brown teals'.

'A wander of grey teals' was inspired by the travelling habits of this bird. Their preferred habitats are freshwater lakes and lagoons, but if their home pond starts to dry up, they will travel great distances in search of water.

Black teals are diving ducks, which float on the surface before suddenly plunging underwater in search of food. They are capable of covering large distances while submerged, and flocks of them can be called 'a splash of black teals'.

Paradise shelducks are large, noisy ducks, so 'a flap of paradise shelducks' refers to their loud nature.

Fernbirds are notoriously cryptic and can go completely unnoticed. Perfectly camouflaged amongst their favoured scrubby habitat, they only occasionally make calls, so they are 'a secret of fernbirds'.

The collective nouns for two crake species are also based on their secretive nature: 'a rumour of marsh crakes' and 'a sneaking of spotless crakes'.

Banded rails have similar characteristics — they barely venture out from hiding in vegetation, but when they do they can be called 'a skulk of banded rails'.

In similar habitats you may find New Zealand dabchicks, small diving birds which have an amazing ability to change their buoyancy by altering the way their feathers are held against their body. 'A float of dabchicks' is a nice way to describe them.

Around the coastline of Aotearoa, little shags can be seen perching on wharves and other structures that give them a vantage point and somewhere to dry their feathers. Their distribution is widespread but patchy, hence 'a staggering of little shags'.

Pied shags are similar in colouring to little shags, but are larger. When they dive for prey in harbours or estuaries their bodies are completely submerged and resemble a snorkel, so 'a snorkelling of pied shags' is a reference to that.

Spotted shags are known to gather in their thousands, and 'an assembly of spotted shags' reflects the way they stand almost motionless as a group.

King shags are a much rarer species, found only in the Marlborough Sounds. 'A throne of king shags' relates to the way they roost on elevated vantage points and also is a nod to the royal aspect of their name.

Our most common heron species, white-faced herons can most often be seen at the seashore slowly wading through water, sneaking up on their prey — thus 'a creeping of white-faced herons'.

A small bird that often goes unnoticed around our coastlines is the pipit. The collective noun 'a seed of pipits' was chosen for poetic reasons, because they are small and seeds make up part of their diet.

Wrybills are dainty shorebirds that perform synchronised flight displays in large flocks. If they spy a threat, they all take flight, moving in harmony to create one large entity: 'a rhythm of wrybills'.

In the South Island, wrybills share a similar habitat to the black stilt, a rare, long-legged bird with striking black colouring. 'An elevation of black stilts' relates to their long legs, and also to the fact that their population has been elevated thanks to great conservation efforts.

Pied stilts are much more common than black stilts and are slightly taller. They gather in large groups, often standing on one leg, so 'a tilt of pied stilts' seems fitting.

On the seashore, if a New Zealand dotterel senses a threat it will perform a display of distraction, leading intruders away from its nest or chicks. Its collective noun is therefore 'a distraction'.

Banded dotterels are slightly smaller than New Zealand dotterels and are fast runners, especially when they are young. They have a foraging style which consists of intermittent bursts of sprinting, earning them the noun 'a scurry of banded dotterels'.

Oystercatchers always seem to be in a hurry to get somewhere, so 'a rush of variable oystercatchers' and 'a dash of South Island pied oystercatchers' reflect the way they sprint across the seashore.

Australasian gannets often forage in large groups, and are famous for their fishing technique, in which they dive into the ocean at great speeds. 'A plummet of Australasian gannets' makes perfect sense to describe this behaviour.

Caspian terns hunt in a similar way but closer to the seashore. They can be distinguished from other tern species by their large size, but also their posture — they are frequently looking downwards, scoping their surroundings for any potential prey, so you may see 'a survey of Caspian terns'.

Fairy terns are a much smaller tern species, and are currently considered our rarest bird. Because of their dainty size and small population, a 'wisp of fairy terns' seems an appropriate collective noun.

Cape petrels are small seabird, which frequently follow fishing boats, foraging for food scraps. In large groups they make chattery calls together and will squabble over food, so 'a quarrel of Cape petrels' is a good way to describe a group of these distinctively coloured birds.

Another small seabird, the fairy prion, are numerous — their population is estimated to be in the millions, although sadly much of their breeding habitat has been lost due to habitat destruction and the introduction of predators. Because of their light blue colouring, large population size and tendency to gather in large flocks, 'a sky of fairy prions' is fitting.

An even smaller seabird, the New Zealand storm petrel — thought to be extinct until it was rediscovered in 2003 — seems to walk on water, the birds using their long legs to effortlessly glide over the surface of the ocean while foraging. Their collective noun is 'a skittering of storm petrels'.

Sooty shearwaters are a common seabird that gather in large numbers. Flocks of these dark-coloured birds look like a cloud of smoke hanging over the ocean, so it seems appropriate their collective noun is 'a haze'.

Likewise, the light-mantled sooty albatross is a smoky colour rather than being pure white like most albatross species. The collective noun 'a brume' means mist or fog.

Albatrosses are usually solitary birds, but when the opportunity to feed presents itself, many different species will gather together to feast. The collective nouns for albatrosses and mollymawks in this book reflect their effortless flying skills, such as 'a gliding of antipodean albatrosses' and 'a soaring of white-capped mollymawks'.

Penguins spend a lot of time at sea, their bodies perfectly suited to gliding through the ocean, but when they come ashore their walking styles are less than elegant. The collective nouns for the following penguins were invented to reflect the almost comical way they walk on land: 'a strolling of Fiordland crested penguins', 'a shuffling of erect-crested penguins' and 'a plodding of yellow-eyed penguins'.

Although a lot of our native birds are now only found in remote locations and sanctuaries, many can be found closer to home — in your local reserves and gardens — if you know what to look and listen for. I hope by reading this book you'll not only appreciate the illustrations and enjoy the collective nouns, but also find a new bird you may not have known about.

I believe that illustrations are the best way to show these beautiful birds, as opposed to photographs. Often with photography, identifying features can be hidden, and it's very hard to get clear photos of birds together in a group. Illustrations are widely used in bird identification guides, as they give a great overview of a bird's appearance. I loved creating the images of these beautiful birds which accompany the collective nouns.

You may have noticed there is an order to the birds featured in this book: from birds which are classified 'not threatened' to the most endangered (the fairy tern). The sad reality is that all of our native bird species are under threat in some way, whether it's because their habitats are diminishing, their nests are being destroyed by introduced pests, or climate change is affecting their food sources.

There are snippets of information about each bird at the end of this book, to provide some insight into their conservation status and where you can find them. I hope you enjoy these collective nouns and have the opportunity to use them next time you are out in the wild.

A banditry of tomtits
He pāhuanga miromiro

An asylum of shining cuckoos

He whareheahea pīpīwhārauroa

A battalion of swamp harriers

He hokowhitu kāhu

A gossiping of yellow-crowned parakeets

He ngutungutu kākāriki

A creeping of white-faced herons

He koropuku matuku moana

A fall of grey warblers
He hinganga riroriro

A loft of New Zealand pigeons

He hekenga kererū

A scavenging of black-backed gulls

He whakaanganga karoro

A spiral of brown creepers
He kōmiro pīpipi

A plummet of Australasian gannets
He tirikōhunga tākapu

An echo of moreporks
He pāorooro ruru

A wander of grey teals

He āmionga tētē moroiti

A ringing of bellbirds
He tīorooro korimako

A splash of black teals

He paratī pāpango

A tilt of pied stilts
He tikoki poaka

A staggering of little shags

He hīrorirori kawau paka

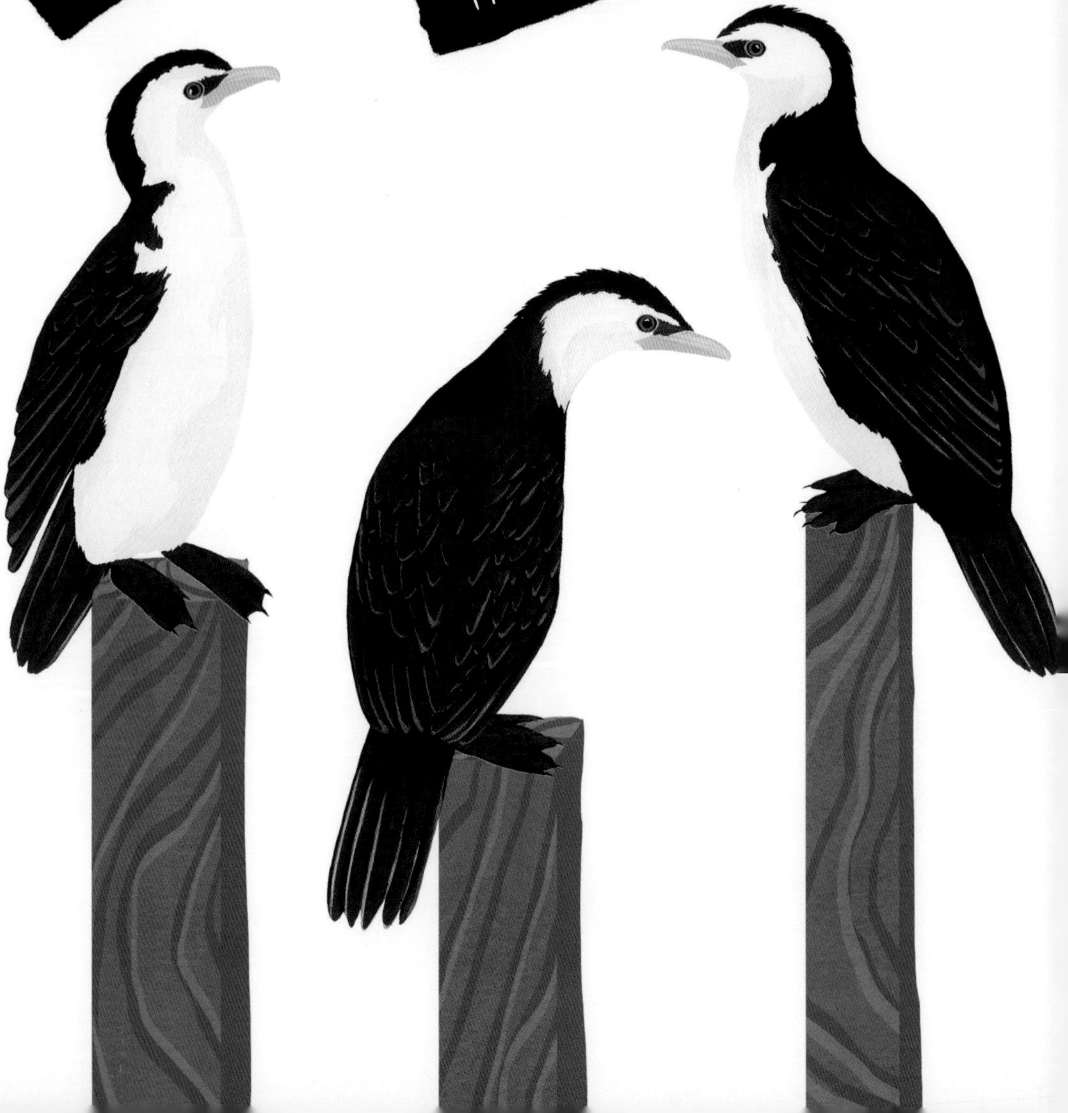

A swoop of welcome swallows
He kurutohitohi warou

A gawky of pūkeko

He whētētē pūkeko

An ecstasy of tūī

He manawarū tūī

An assembly of spotted shags

He whakaminenga pārekareka

A flutter of fantails

He pererū pīwakawaka

A rattle of sacred kingfishers

He kākaranga kōtare

A flap of paradise shelducks

He hāngengangenga pūtangitangi

A spectacle of silvereyes

He inā-rawa tauhou

A quarrel of Cape petrels

He totohe pāpangao

A weight of royal albatrosses

He taimahatanga toroa

A covert of Australian coots

He kuhunga tētē-whero

A flight of black shags
He rerenga kawau pango

A measurement of royal spoonbills

He inenga kōtuku ngutupapa

A cackling of red-crowned parakeets

He ketekete kākāriki

A sky of fairy prions
He rangi tītī wainui

A dabbling of brown teals
He kokoti pāteke

A haunting of North Island kōkako

He taipōnga kōkako

A scurrying of little spotted kiwi

He takawhitinga kiwi pukupuku

A distraction of New Zealand dotterels

He whakawārenga tūturiwhatu

A jubilee of New Zealand falcons

He tiupirī kārearea

A loot of weka

He pāhuanga weka

A siren of saddlebacks

He tīoronga tīeke

A rush of variable oystercatchers

He rere tōrea pango

A float of dabchicks
He māūnunga weweia

A bolt of yellowheads

He hiko mohua

A snorkeling of pied shags
He rukunga kāruhiruhi

A raft of little blue penguins

He mōkihi kororā

A skulk of banded rails
He konihi mioweka

A brume of light-mantled sooty albatrosses

He piātanga toroa haunui

A rumour of marsh crakes
He waha kaunga koitareke

A committee of white-fronted terns

He komiti tara

A chime of riflemen

He tātangi titipounamu

A sneaking of spotless crakes

He torohe pūweto

A foraging of North Island brown kiwi

He hamuhamu kiwi

A secret of fernbirds
He tauhanga mātātā

A dash of South Island pied oystercatchers

He taitai tōrea tuawhenua

A company of South Island robins
He kamupene kakaruwai

A pantheon of bar-tailed godwits

He manomano kuaka

A seed of pipits

He kākano pīhoihoi

A shuffling of erect-crested penguins

He hōnekeneke tawaki

A squabble of red-billed gulls

He totohenga tarāpunga

A cloud of whiteheads

He hākiwakiwa pōpokotea

A haze of sooty shearwaters

He kauruki tītī

A rally of North Island robins

He whakaaraara toutouwai

A soaring of white-capped mollymawks

He hāronga toroa whakatopatopa

A tussock of South Island takahē

He wīwī takahē

A skittering of New Zealand storm petrels

He heahea takahikare-moana

A rustling of rowi

He ngaehe rowi

A hive of stitchbirds

He hangai hihi

A rhythm of wrybills

He whakataki ngutu parore

A whistling of whio

He whiowhionga whio

He kōtītiti kākā
A hoon of kākā

A rummaging of great spotted kiwi

He paraketunga roaroa

A survey of Caspian terns

A scurry of banded dotterels

He takawhiti tūturiwhatu

A strolling of Fiordland crested penguins

He haerēre tawaki

A throne of king shags
He torona kawau pāteketeke

A burrowing of southern brown kiwi

He tāruanga tokoeka

A scattering of reef herons

He horaina tīkāka

A cotillion of black-fronted terns

He kanikani tara pirohe

A plodding of yellow-eyed penguins

He āmaranga hoiho

A circus of kea
He maninirau kea

A flicker of rock wren

He kōpura hurupounamu

A gliding of Antipodean albatrosses
He tītipinga toroa o te moana nui a Kiwa

A chattering of orange-fronted parakeets
He kōrerorereronga kākāriki karaka

A gullery of black-billed gulls

He hīkarawaka tarāpuka

A glide of Salvin's mollymawks

He terenga kautuku

A freeze of Australasian bitterns

He tīōnga matuku-hūrepo

A shadow of black robins
He ātārangi kakaruia

A booming of kākāpō

He ngunguru kākāpō

A pose of white herons

He hahakenga kōtuku

An elevation of black stilts

He hikinga kakī

A stand of shore plovers

He tūranga tuturuatu

A wisp of fairy terns
He tūtutupō tara iti

About the Birds

Not Threatened

The tomtit/miromiro is a small, territorial forest bird. Their diet consists mainly of insects and they are generally found in pairs or family groups. Male tomtits have distinctive black and white plumage, whereas the females and juveniles are less bold, with brown and white colouring. They have a stable population that resides in patches of forest throughout the North and South islands. 'A banditry of tomtits' is adapted from the collective noun for the small North American bird the titmouse.*

Shining cuckoos/pīpīwhārauroa are migratory birds that visit New Zealand in spring to lay their eggs in the nests of grey warblers, before leaving the eggs to hatch and be raised by the unsuspecting foster parents. They are common throughout New Zealand wherever grey warblers are found. Their distinctive alarm-like call is commonly heard, but their elusive nature means they aren't often seen. 'An asylum of shining cuckoos' is adapted from the existing collective noun for cuckoos.

Swamp harriers/kāhu are a common sight soaring in the sky above farmland and wetlands. They are large birds of prey and can often be seen on the roadside, taking advantage of roadkill. 'A battalion of swamp harriers' is adapted from the existing collective noun for harriers.

Yellow-crowned parakeets/kākāriki are small, chatty and colourful birds found on offshore islands and in some mainland forests. They are the most common of all the parakeets and have bright green plumage. Their chatter-like calls often give away their location, as they are well camouflaged amongst foliage.

White-faced herons/matuku moana are the most common heron in New Zealand. They can be seen in estuaries and other wetland habitats where they slowly and meticulously stalk

* The source for all existing collective nouns is www.nzbirds.com

their prey. They nest high on tree tops, usually in large trees with water nearby.

Grey warblers/riroriro are our second-smallest birds. They are the targets of the parasitic shining cuckoo, which lays a single egg in the warblers' nest for the warblers to raise as if it were their own. 'A fall of grey warblers' is adapted from the existing collective noun for warblers.

New Zealand pigeons/kererū are one of two native New Zealand pigeons (the other is the Chatham Island pigeon). They are known for their hefty size and occasionally clumsy antics. They can be found in forests throughout the country, where they feast on berries and are therefore a key disperser of the seeds of many native trees. Kererū will sometimes travel long distances for a reliable food source. 'A loft of New Zealand pigeons' is adapted from the existing collective noun for pigeons.

Black-backed gulls/karoro are one of the most common large birds in New Zealand. They can be found in a range of habitats from the seashore to farmland, and are both predators and scavengers. Karoro congregate together in large flocks when feeding and roosting. 'A scavenging of black-backed gulls' is adapted from the existing collective noun for gulls.

Brown creepers/pīpipi are social forest birds only found in the South Island and Stewart Island. Related to the yellowhead and whitehead, they can be found in tree canopies in large, chatty flocks. They can often be seen hanging upside down from trees in search of insects and fruit. 'A spiral of brown creepers' is adapted from the existing collective noun for creepers.

Australasian gannets/tākapu are large seabirds known for their distinctive diving technique, plummeting into the ocean at high speed to catch fish. They are social birds, gathering in groups to forage for food and to form large breeding colonies.

Moreporks/ruru are our only surviving endemic owls. They are capable of flying almost silently to sneak up on their prey and have amazing eyesight and hearing, which enables them to hunt in darkness for insects, small mammals and birds. In forests and tree-dense suburbs, their distinctive call can be heard at night, often as counter-calling to establish territorial boundaries amongst males.

Grey teals/tētē moroiti are small ducks found throughout New Zealand in freshwater lakes, lagoons and swamps, where they feed mostly at night, on insects and molluscs. Grey teals are nomadic, which means they can take advantage of newly flooded areas and will travel large distances in search of suitable habitat.

Bellbirds/korimako are famous for their melodic calls, which sound like bells chiming. They are widespread throughout the country but are more common in the South Island. When they gather together in food-rich areas they produce an amazing collective sound. Male bellbirds are olive-green, while the females are a duller olive-brown with a distinctive white cheek stripe.

Black teal/pāpango are diving ducks known for their 'rubber-duck' body shape and seemingly effortless buoyancy. They gather in large flocks and spend a lot of time underwater foraging for food. Male teal have piercing yellow eyes and are black and green in colour, whereas the females are mostly brown.

Pied stilts/poaka are a common sight at estuaries, wetlands and coastal areas. Their black and white colouring and long red legs make them unmistakeable. They gather in flocks throughout the year, often with other species of wading birds, but are wary of people and will usually fly away yapping when approached.

Little shags/kawaupaka are the smallest of all New Zealand's shag species and are found throughout the county in coastal and freshwater habitats. They forage individually but nest in colonies, often with other shag species. They can be seen perched on vantage points, drying their feathers and on the lookout for food.

Welcome swallows/warou are small, elegant birds known for their acrobatic flight displays. Widespread and abundant throughout New Zealand, especially around coastal and wetland areas, they can be seen gathering in large flocks, perched on fixed structures or flying together hawking insects. 'A swoop of welcome swallows' is adapted from the existing collective noun for swallows.

Pūkeko are common, easily recognisable birds with distinctive blue and red colouring. Wetlands with areas of vegetation are their preferred habitat, but they can often be seen in farm paddocks. They live in groups with a complicated social structure, sharing a communal nest, in which eggs from multiple birds are laid. Once they hatch, all group members contribute towards feeding and raising the chicks. 'A gawky of pukeko' is an existing term.

Tūī are one of our most recognisable birds, with their iridescent plumage, unique throat tuft (poi) and melodic and varied song. Tūī are talented vocalists; they sing elaborate compositions of bell-like notes, coughs, grunts and whistles, often singing in pairs or groups. Tūī are found throughout most of the country in forests and suburban areas.

Spotted shags/pārekareka are a yellow-footed marine shag species endemic to New Zealand. Their breeding plumage is spectacular, with bright skin around the eyes, a head crest, and black spots at the tips of their feathers. They are found mostly in the South Island, where they congregate in large numbers; during breeding season, colonies may be as large as 700 pairs.

Fantails/pīwakawaka are familiar and common birds found throughout the country. Their distinctive fanned tail, constant chatter and friendly nature means they are adored by many people. They are found in forests, scrubland and gardens, often in the company of other bird species that they follow, chasing insects disturbed by the other birds' movements. Fantails have two colour morphs: the more common pied morph and a black morph, which mostly occurs in the South Island.

Sacred kingfishers/kōtare are a familiar sight around estuaries and wetlands. They are often seen perching high on a vantage point scoping for a wide range of prey, which can include lizards, crabs, insects and even mice. Kingfishers have brilliant colouring and are widespread throughout the country in a variety of habitats. 'A rattle of kingfishers' is adapted from the existing collective noun for kingfishers.

Paradise shelducks/pūtangitangi are common large and noisy ducks. They are New Zealand's most widespread waterfowl species and often gather in large flocks. They are unusual in the bird world in that the female is more eye-catching than the male, with white heads and chestnut bodies compared to the males' mostly black colouring.

Silvereyes/tauhou are small, colourful birds found all over the county in habitats including gardens, orchards and forests. They are one of New Zealand's most abundant bird species and one of the most recognisable, with their olive-green colouring and white eye-ring. They are noisy when foraging for food in flocks, which during winter can become quite numerous. 'A spectacle of silvereyes' is an existing term.

Cape petrels/pāpangao are small, distinctively-coloured seabirds regularly seen off the coast of New Zealand, especially south of Cook Strait. They gather in groups, often with birds much larger than themselves, and follow fishing vessels in search of scraps. They are quite noisy when squabbling over food and also during nesting season.

At Risk

Royal albatrosses/toroa are one of the largest albatross species. Their wingspan exceeds three metres and they weigh around nine kilograms. They breed only once every two years, as it takes almost a whole year to raise a single chick. They are generally solitary at sea but gather around fishing vessels to take advantage of food scraps. Their powerful sense of smell means they can detect food many kilometres away. 'A weight of royal albatrosses' is adapted from the existing collective noun for albatrosses.

Australian coots are recent arrivals to New Zealand — they were first recorded breeding here in the 1950s — but have established themselves as a native species. They are a waterbird with duck-like features, and fill the niche of the extinct native coot. They are patchily distributed around the country and rely on freshwater habitat with plenty of vegetation for food. 'A covert of Australian coots' is adapted from the existing collective noun for coots.

● **Black shags/kawau pango** are found in estuaries and harbours, often near cities or towns. Although they are widely distributed throughout New Zealand, their population is sparse. They are our largest shag species and are usually solitary, except in areas where food is plentiful, in which case they will gather in large flocks to forage. 'A flight of black shags' is adapted from the existing collective noun for cormorants.

● **The royal spoonbill/kōtuku ngutupapa** is a large wading bird with a distinctive long, spoon-shaped black bill. They use their bill to scoop up food in shallow freshwater habitats. Their population has increased since self-introducing to New Zealand from Australia, and they can occasionally be seen at estuaries in small groups. 'A measurement of royal spoonbills' is adapted from the existing collective noun for spoonbills.

● **Red-crowned parakeets/kākāriki** are mid-sized, brightly coloured parakeets with distinctive red crowns. Predation by introduced pests has seen them lost from the mainland of New Zealand, apart from fenced sanctuaries. On some offshore islands, however, they gather in flocks and communicate with chatter-like calls.

● **Fairy prions/tītī wainui** are small, blue-grey seabirds common in the oceans surrounding New Zealand. Before the introduction of predators, they likely bred on the New Zealand mainland, but they now breed only on a few offshore islands. Fairy prions gather in large flocks at sea, where they capture prey from the ocean surface or by making shallow dives.

● **Brown teals/pāteke** are dabbling ducks that live in wet forests, swamps, estuaries, small streams and ponds. Once widespread, their population plummeted with the introduction of predators to New Zealand, but conservation management has seen their numbers recovering on offshore islands and in mainland sanctuaries. Brown teals usually live in pairs or flocks and are most active at twilight and at night.

● **North Island kōkako** are known as 'grey ghosts' due to their elusive nature. They perform beautiful songs and duets, which consist of haunting notes and bell-like tones. They are poor fliers, instead using their strong legs to hop from branch to branch in search of leaves and fruit to eat. Kōkako are rare and only found in native broadleaf forests, where they rely on predator control for their survival.

● Little spotted kiwi/pukupuku are the smallest of our kiwi species, at only 30 centimetres long. Like all kiwi they are flightless and nocturnal. They were once widespread throughout New Zealand, but their vulnerability to introduced predators has driven them close to extinction; they survive now only on offshore islands and in mainland sanctuaries. Their entire population originates from only seven birds left alive in the early 1900s, which means they have very low genetic diversity.

● New Zealand dotterels/tūturiwhatu are shorebirds found mostly in the North Island and on Stewart Island. They are threatened by human disturbance and coastal development, but their vulnerable nesting sites are often protected by local community groups. When their nesting sites are threatened, dotterel parents perform distraction displays to lead any potential predator away from their nest. After breeding, they gather at estuaries in large flocks before returning to nesting sites the following season.

● New Zealand falcons/kārearea are fast-flying raptors, capable of high speeds when pursuing prey in flight. Their wings are broad, allowing them to quickly manoeuvre through dense native forests. They are widespread but rare, as they face many threats including predation by feral cats, pigs and possums and lack of suitable habitat due to forest clearing. Male falcons are much smaller than females, but both sexes are capable of catching prey much larger than themselves. 'A jubilee of falcons' is adapted from the existing collective noun for falcons.

● Weka are curious flightless birds found in a range of habitats. They are friendly, often approaching people, and as opportunistic scavengers will often search human belongings and steal any food they can. Their population fluctuates as they are vulnerable to drought as well as introduced predators. They are considered to be 'recovering', as predator control is helping their population increase.

● Saddlebacks/tīeke are noisy and active forest birds which have a wide range of calls, including loud alerts as well as gentle, flute-like sounds. Although still rare, both North and South Island species have recovered from critically low populations thanks to intensive conservation work. They can be abundant in areas free of predators such as islands and mainland sanctuaries. They forage in family groups, using their strong bills to hack away at tree bark and rotten logs to access grubs and other insects.

● Variable oystercatchers/tōrea pango are distinctive birds commonly seen around coastal areas. They usually nest on beaches, where they are vulnerable to human disturbance and predation, but they have benefited from areas being managed to protect other rare species. During nesting season they are highly territorial, but young birds gather in flocks at estuaries over winter.

● New Zealand dabchicks/weweia are small grebes. They are patchily distributed throughout the North Island and are rarer in the South Island. They can be found at small lakes and inlets, where they can stay underwater for up to 30 seconds in search of food. Dabchicks have the ability to change their buoyancy by altering the direction of their feathers in relation to their body, enabling them to fully submerge themselves underwater.

● Yellowheads/mohua are small, colourful and social songbirds related to the whitehead and brown creeper. They used to be common and widespread in the South Island before the introduction of pests like ship rats, but now only isolated populations remain. Translocations to southern predator-free islands have helped establish successful populations, where large flocks of them can be seen foraging high in the treetops.

● Pied shags/kāruhiruhi are large shags found around New Zealand. They favour coastal waters but occasionally forage in estuaries and freshwater locations. They face a variety of threats, including commercial fishing and felling of the trees that provide their nesting sites. There is some evidence that their population is declining at the top and bottom of the country but recovering in central New Zealand.

● Little blue penguins/kororā are the world's smallest penguin species. They are the most common penguin species in New Zealand and are found in many places around the coast. They face dangers such as attacks from dogs and introduced pests, as well as the risk of being caught in fishing nets. They feed at sea as solitary individuals or in small groups during the day, then at night return to shore, frequently in a group known as a raft. 'A raft of little blue penguins' is adapted from the existing collective noun for penguins.

● Banded rails/mioweka are wetland birds that are experts in remaining unseen. The draining and destruction of wetland habits and introduction of pests means many populations have disappeared from the mainland of New Zealand but small and scattered groups remain. They are capable of flying long distances and have been known to venture far from their breeding sites.

● Light-mantled sooty albatrosses/toroa haunui are elegant and distinctly dark-coloured seabirds. They breed in the subantarctic islands in large but distanced groups, and pairs raise a single chick every two years. Their population is threatened by commercial fishing and feral predators at some breeding islands.

● Marsh crakes/koitareke are tiny, extremely secretive wetland birds which are rarely seen. Little is known about their population, but they are widespread in remaining wetland habitats. They are threatened by extensive loss of habitat from wetland drainage as well as predation by cats, stoats and dogs.

● White-fronted terns/tara are a familiar sight around New Zealand coastlines. They are the most common of our terns and flocks of them can sometimes number in the thousands. Despite this, their overall population is declining due to nesting colonies being predated by introduced pests and other birds such as gulls, as well as disturbance by dogs and humans. 'A committee of white-fronted terns' is adapted from the existing collective noun for terns.

● The rifleman/titipounamu is our smallest native bird, weighing only six grams. The males are bright green and are slightly smaller than the females, which have streaky brown plumage. They can be found in remnant patches of mature forest, where they scour the trees in search of insects. They have a range of extremely high-pitched, echo-like calls, some of which are beyond the range of human hearing. 'A chime of riflemen' is adapted from the existing collective noun for wrens.

● **Spotless crakes/pūweto** are small wetland birds which are rarely seen. They favour freshwater habitats with plenty of vegetation, which they rarely venture far from. Much of the birds' habitat has been lost due to the draining of wetlands, and introduced predators have also had an impact on their population. Because of their elusive nature, an accurate estimation of their population size cannot be made, although they are more common in the North Island.

● **North Island brown kiwi** are the only kiwi with a natural wild population in the North Island. They suffer from predation by stoats, dogs and ferrets, and habitat loss, but can become common in areas with predator control.

● **Fernbirds/mātātā** are small, streaky brown, long-tailed birds found in dense wetland vegetation and dry shrubland. Populations of fernbirds have been lost due to wetland drainage and the usual array of predators. They remain only in scattered locations, but translocations have been successful in establishing new populations in secure habitats.

● **South Island pied oystercatchers/tōrea** are the most abundant oystercatcher species in New Zealand. They differ from the variable oystercatcher by having more white in their plumage. They typically can be found at estuaries over summer before they retreat inland to rivers in the South Island for breeding season.

● **South Island robins/kakaruwai** are small birds found in mature forest and scrub throughout the South Island. Robins that live in popular walking or tramping areas can become quite friendly towards humans and will often approach and follow them on walking tracks, preying on any bugs that may be stirred up by their footsteps. Robins have a patchy distribution but can be common in areas of ideal habitat that are free of introduced predators.

● **Bar-tailed godwits/kuaka** are migratory birds that undertake a non-stop, nine-day, 11,000 kilometre journey from Alaska to New Zealand in the southern spring every year. Once they arrive they gather at estuaries, where they forage mostly for polychaetes (marine worms). The global godwit population is declining due to habitat loss and lack of availability of food sources caused by climate change.

'A pantheon of bar-tailed godwits' is adapted from the existing collective noun for godwits.

● Pipits/pīhoihoi are slender, dainty birds found in widespread open habitat including coasts, grassland, farmland, roadsides, dry river beds, sand dunes and open woodland. Their widespread population is declining in areas of changing habitat, including the draining of wetlands, and on some offshore islands rats have decimated numbers. Pipits are usually seen singly or in pairs, but are occasionally gather in large flocks outside the breeding season.

● Erect-crested penguins/tawaki are mid-sized penguins distinguished by their upright yellow crests and black and white plumage. As they live in remote locations in the subantarctic islands, little is known about their behaviour and population size, but their numbers are thought to be declining due to a reduction in food sources.

● Red-billed gulls/tarāpunga are the most plentiful gull in New Zealand, and are distinctive with their white and pale grey plumage, bright red bill and matching feet. They are most commonly found in coastal areas, where they have a variable diet with krill being the primary food source during breeding season. They nest in large colonies, some of which have been declining rapidly in recent years partly due to falling krill populations. 'A squabble of red-billed gulls' is adapted from the existing collective noun for gulls.

● Whiteheads/pōpokotea are social and chatty songbirds. They are the North Island counterpart of the yellowhead and brown creeper, and similarly, they forage in large, noisy flocks. Whiteheads can be found high in the tree canopies of tall, dense forests, where they hang acrobatically to access hard-to-reach insects. In areas with minimal pests they can become quite numerous, but their population has suffered greatly from habitat loss and predation by introduced mammals.

● Sooty shearwaters/tītī are common seabirds that can gather in flocks of tens of thousands of birds. Despite their large population size — an estimated 21 million birds — they face threats such as being killed by fishery operations as well as introduced pests, which have decimated most mainland breeding colonies.

North Island robins/toutouwai are friendly, ground-foraging birds found in scattered populations throughout mature forest and scrublands. Robins are known for their trusting nature and will often approach people in areas that are frequented by walkers. Their population initially declined due to forest clearance and the arrival of mammalian pests, but has since been boosted by translocations to pest-free islands and mainland sanctuaries.

White-capped mollymawks/toroa whakatopatopa are the largest of our mollymawks. They are ocean birds and can be seen following fishing vessels, scavenging for scraps. They are the most common albatross to fall victim to fishery bycatch, and their population is declining.

Threatened – Nationally Vulnerable

South Island takahē are a large, flightless member of the rail family that live in grassland habitat. They were thought to be extinct before a surviving population in the Murchison Mountains was rediscovered in the 1940s. Populations of takahē have been established by successful translocation to various offshore islands and mainland sanctuaries around the country. All takahē in New Zealand are the South Island species, as the North Island species is extinct. 'A tussock of takahē' is an existing term.

New Zealand storm petrels/takahikare-moana are small, dainty seabirds that were thought to be extinct until they were rediscovered in the early 2000s off the Coromandel Peninsula. Storm petrels gather food by skimming the surface of the ocean, seemingly walking on water. Their population size is undetermined but may number in the hundreds or thousands.

Rowi are the rarest of all the kiwi species. Once widespread in both the North and South islands, their only natural wild populations have been reduced to the west coast of the South Island. Their population was at its lowest at around 160 birds, but conservation efforts have seen that number increase, and birds have since been translocated to offshore islands for breeding programmes.

● Stitchbirds/hihi are rare forest birds. At one time reduced to a single remnant population due to predation by introduced pests, they have since made a comeback thanks to intensive management, and can now be found in a number of mainland and island sanctuaries. Male stitchbirds have striking black, white and yellow plumage, whereas females are brown with patches of yellow and white.

● Wrybills/ngutu parore are tiny shorebirds, often seen gathering in large flocks at estuaries where they perform mesmerising, rhythmic flight displays. They are the only bird in the world with a bill that curves sideways, always to the right — it allows them to reach under river stones for food. They breed exclusively in the South Island but spend their winters in harbours in the upper North Island. Their population appears to be declining.

● Blue ducks/whio are large ducks that live in clean, fast-flowing, high-altitude rivers in both the North and South islands. Male whio whistle, whereas the females' call is lower and raspier. Poor water quality and predation by stoats, especially of nesting females, are the main causes of their population decline. 'A whistling of whio' is an existing term.

● Kākā are large bush parrots found in forest remnants and sanctuaries around New Zealand. They are noisy, cheeky and confident around humans. Forest clearance has been a factor in their population decline, but the main cause is predation by mammalian predators, especially stoats.

● Great spotted kiwi/roaroa are the second-largest of all our kiwi species. In the wild they live only in the northwest of the South Island. While foraging, they remain in contact with their mate by calling to each other, and will become aggressive if another kiwi ventures into their territory. Habitat loss and predation by stoats are the main causes of their threatened status.

● Caspian terns/taranui are the largest tern species found in New Zealand, and are distinguishable by their size and heavy-set, bright red bill. They are widespread but not very common. Their nesting sites are also vulnerable to destruction by people, dogs and vehicles. They are solitary hunters but gather together to roost.

Banded dotterels/tūturiwhatu are dainty shorebirds found around the coast of New Zealand. They have a characteristic foraging technique that includes short bursts of running to catch prey. They are ground-nesting birds, which makes them very vulnerable to predator attacks and disturbance by human activity.

Fiordland crested penguins/tawaki are tall, secretive birds that breed along the rugged coast of southern New Zealand. Their population is declining due to adult birds being caught as by-catch in fishery operations, as well as human disturbance to nesting sites, predation by stoats and dog attacks. During the breeding season they gather in colonies, and once their chicks are old enough they stay together in a crèche while their parents are out at sea in search of food.

Threatened — Nationally Endangered

King shags/kawau pāteketeke are the rarest shag species in the world. They are found only in the Marlborough Sounds and, because of this, their entire population is at risk should a disaster such as a devastating weather event or oil spill occur. King shags are expert divers — they feed on fish found near the ocean floor. When on land they roost together in groups.

Southern brown kiwi/tokoeka are the largest of all the kiwi species. They are generally nocturnal but on Stewart Island can sometimes be seen foraging during the day. Their population has declined due to habitat loss and predation by dogs and other mammalian pests, but they can be numerous in forest areas where pests are controlled.

Reef herons/tīkāka are patchily distributed around the coast of New Zealand. They are less approachable than other heron species. Their population is estimated to be in the hundreds but is thought to be stable. Reef herons are well camouflaged in their coastal surroundings. They slowly creep through shallow water to stalk small fish and crustaceans. 'A scattering of reef herons' is adapted from the existing collective noun for herons.

● Black-fronted terns/tara pirohe are small birds found mostly in the South Island and only occasionally seen in the North Island. Adults are distinguishable from other small terns by their bold orange bill, black cap and darker grey wings. Black-fronted terns breed in colonies in South Island braided rivers and estuaries, where they are susceptible to attacks by introduced mammals and birds, and threatened by the recreational use of rivers. 'A cotillion of black-fronted terns' is adapted from the existing collective noun for terns.

● Yellow-eyed penguins/hoiho are the rarest penguin species in the world. They are tall penguins distinguishable by their yellow head feathers and, of course, their yellow eyes. They nest in coastal forests, choosing sites with plenty of vegetation. They face many threats, including habitat loss, predation, being caught in commercial fishing nets, human disturbance and disease.

● Kea are an alpine parrot species. They are friendly and confident birds that are famous for their inquisitive nature and destructive antics. In the twentieth century, kea were condemned as sheep killers by farmers, who culled huge numbers before the birds were given protected status. Kea are highly intelligent; they utilise skilled foraging techniques and social hierarchies are recorded within flocks. They have shown adaptability to their changing habitat but still face threats such as introduced predators.

● Rock wrens/hurupounamu are small, alpine-dwelling birds. They are capable of flight, but prefer to hop around on rocks, flicking their wings and bobbing their heads when they move. Rock wrens build nests in cavities at ground level, making their eggs and chicks highly vulnerable to mice and stoats.

● *Threatened – Nationally Critical*

● Antipodean albatrosses/toroa are one of the largest albatross species found in New Zealand waters. They are long-lived birds that spend most of their lives at sea, coming ashore only to breed every two years. Like other albatross species, they are scavengers and frequently follow fishing vessels seeking scraps, resulting in many being caught and killed by long-lines. Climate change has also reduced the amount of available natural food, contributing to population decline.

● Orange-fronted parakeets/kākāriki karaka are the rarest of all our native parakeets. Once widespread, they now survive only in pockets of beech forest in the South Island and on some offshore islands. These small parakeets nest in tree cavities and are vulnerable to mammalian predators, especially in years following beech masts (mass-seeding events), when predator numbers surge. Conservation efforts striving to keep these birds from extinction include intensive pest management and captive breeding programmes. 'A chattering of orange-fronted parakeets' is adapted from the existing collective noun for parakeets.

● Black-billed gulls/tarāpuka are gulls that reside mostly in the South Island. They nest mainly in inland rivers and streams in large numbers, but are very vulnerable to predators, agricultural practices and lack of food caused by ocean warming. Not only that, but vehicles have been deliberately driven through nesting colonies, destroying chicks, eggs and adults, and there have been instances of adults being shot in large numbers. 'A gullery of black-billed gulls' is adapted from the existing collective noun for gulls.

● Salvin's mollymawks/kautuku are familiar albatrosses in the coastal waters south of Cook Strait, where they frequently pursue fishing vessels in search of discarded scraps. Their scavenging behaviour often leads to them being accidentally caught and killed. Salvin's mollymawks are expert flyers and spend much of their time at sea, coming ashore only to breed.

● Australasian bitterns/matuku-hūrepo are rare, cryptic herons found in wetland areas around New Zealand. Their population has suffered from the draining of wetlands to make way for farmland, as well as declining water quality and a resulting lack of food. When disturbed, a bittern will adopt a frozen pose, with its head pointed directly upwards. This acts as camouflage making it harder to detect, but the bittern can still keep a watchful eye out. 'A freeze of Australasian bitterns' is adapted from the existing collective noun for bitterns.

● Black robins/kakaruia are small, entirely black songbirds native to the Chatham Islands. Because of their conservation story they are one of New Zealand's most well-known birds. They came dangerously close to extinction in the mid-twentieth century, with only five surviving birds, just one of which was female. Innovative conservation techniques saw the black robin escape extinction, and today their population is relatively stable, but has very low genetic diversity.

● Kākāpō is an unusual bird: a large, flightless, nocturnal parrot. Kākāpō were once common all over New Zealand, but their lack of any defences against mammalian predators made them easy prey for introduced pests. Early conservation attempts to transfer kākāpō to predator-free offshore islands in the nineteenth century were unsuccessful, but the technique of translocating kākāpō to safe islands proved to be vital years later. Their population is now slowly increasing with intensive management and monitoring. 'A booming of kākāpō' is an existing term.

● White herons/kōtuku, although well known, are rare in New Zealand. Elegant, with pure white plumage, they have long legs that enable them to wade through estuaries. They have only one breeding site in New Zealand, located in Westland, which makes them vulnerable should any catastrophic event occur there. 'A pose of white herons' is adapted from the existing collective noun for herons.

● Black stilts/kakī are the world's rarest wading bird. They are elegant and long-legged, with black plumage, and live in South Island braided riders and wetlands. They were once widespread around New Zealand but their breeding population is currently confined to the Mackenzie Basin. In the wild most of their eggs and chicks are lost to stoats, feral cats and hedgehogs, so their population is intensively managed in an effort to keep them from extinction. In recent years, a captive breeding programme has seen a large number of captive-raised juveniles being released into the wild.

● Shore plovers/tuturuatu are not only one of New Zealand's rarest birds but also one of the world's rarest shorebirds. Once common on shorelines all around the country, introduced predators drove them to extinction everywhere except the Chatham Islands. They are extremely vulnerable to mammalian pests, as well as natural predators such as black-backed gulls and ruru. Captive breeding programs have helped boost the numbers of these birds and they have been released on some predator-free islands in the hope of establishing new populations. 'A stand of shore plovers' is adapted from the existing collective noun for plovers.

● Fairy terns/tara iti are small coastal terns found only at a few sites north of Auckland. Fairy terns nest in small scrapes in the sand, which makes their eggs and chicks very vulnerable to pests, human disturbance and adverse weather. They are also threatened by habitat destruction due to human development and disruption to their food sources. Their gravely small population is intensively managed by conservationists, especially during breeding season, as every bird's survival is vital to ensuring this species isn't lost forever.

About the Translations

In searching for Māori names of our Aotearoa manu (birds), I scanned through existing publications, some dating back to the early 1900s. I also acknowledge the value of the online Māori Dictionary of New Zealand Birds.

While some manu are known by the same name throughout the motu, many have more than one name in te reo — some having up to five variations. For example, the fantail is known variously as pīwaiwaka, tīwaiwaka, pīrakaraka and tīrakaraka. This book favours the most common names in modern usage.

In the case of the Australian coot and two species of mollymawk, no existing Maori names could be found. In these cases, the species name in English or a distinctive feature was used to find a relative Maori term that could be applied. These novel Maori names are strictly for the purpose of this book alone. Neither I nor the publisher make any claim over naming rights owed to mana whenua for whom these birds are taonga.

Several of the collective nouns in English also do not have immediate corresponding kupu in te reo, such as a 'cotillion' and a 'loft'. For these, the meaning of the English term was used to give the kupu in te reo Maori.

Patricia Tauroa, Ngāpuhi ki Whaingaroa and Ngāti Kahu ki Whaingaroa

About the Author

Melissa Boardman is a Wellington-based illustrator with a passion for New Zealand's native birds. Melissa's illustrations are drawn from her own experiences. She frequently visits sanctuaries and offshore islands, where she spends time observing birds in their natural habitats. Melissa has a deep respect for nature, and enjoys nothing more than being surrounded by trees and birdsong.